TRANSPORT

BRIAN WILLIAMS

Wayland

CONTENTS

4 Introduction

6 The first boats

8 Chariots and carts

10 Ocean-going ships

12 The steam revolution

14 The first railways

16 Balloons and airships

18 Iron ships

First published in 1995 by
Wayland (Publishers) Limited
61 Western Road, Hove, East
Sussex BN3 1JD, England
© Copyright 1995 Wayland
(Publishers) Ltd

British Library Cataloguing in
Publication Data
Williams, Brian
Transport. – (Science Discovery
Series)
I. Title II. Series
388

ISBN 0 7502 1275 6

This book was prepared for
Wayland (Publishers) Limited by
Globe Education
of Nantwich, Cheshire

Concept David Jefferis
Illustrations Alex Pang and Peter Bull
(cover and page 34t)

Printed and bound in Italy by
G. Canale and C.S.p.A., Turin

Acknowledgements

Environmental Picture Library 40
Images back cover
Life File 4
Michael Holford 6b, 11, 12-13, 18
Peter Newark's American Pictures 9,
14-15, 15, 34, 43 Peter Newark's
Historical Pictures 8, 14t, 23, 24b
Quadrant cover (tl, centre and br), 21,
22-23, 24-25, 28, 28-29, 30, 32-33, 35,
40-41, 45
Science Photolibrary 13t, 36, 38, 39,
42, 46-47
Tony Stone 5, 10, 17, 20, 20-21, 29,
30-31, 37
Zefa 6t

388

**This book is to be returned on or before
the last date stamped below.**

X

1 0 FEB 2011

LIBREX

388   R54224F

20 The bicycle

22 The petrol-engined car

24 Into the air

26 Submarines

28 The road revolution

30 Electric and diesel trains

32 Civil aircraft

34 Helicopters

36 Big loaders

38 Rockets and spacecraft

40 Alternative transport

42 Timeline of advance

44 Glossary/1

46 Glossary/2

47 Going further

48 Index

 INTRODUCTION

Humans have been on the move, ever since our first ancestors crossed the plains of Africa, hunting and gathering their food. They travelled on foot, along river valleys, or followed paths made by migrating animals. By the end of the Stone Age, people were trading in flints, amber, salt, and obsidian. These goods were passed along trade routes, some of them hundreds of kilometres long.

About 10,000 years ago people in the Middle East, India and China built the first towns. Farmers sold their crops to townspeople, and for transport they used tame animals, such as asses, to carry loads. Later they harnessed oxen to carts with solid wooden wheels.

Social, economic and military pressures have made people look constantly for new ways of moving themselves and their goods. We do not know who made key inventions, such as the canoe paddle, the sail, or the wheel. They appear in different places, at roughly the same time. Good ideas passed speedily between groups of people and the evolution of writing around 3000 BC made it possible to record details of inventions and pass them on.

◀ Animal transport, like this camel in Pakistan, relies on muscle power. It does not require any alteration to the environment.

▲ Modern transport consumes vast quantities of resources. Besides the energy required to build and power these cars, considerable amounts of materials and energy are required to build the highways, like this highway interchange in the USA.

Today, people want to transport themselves and their goods across continents in hours, not weeks. Technology in partnership with science, human need, and ingenuity backed by money, have created the railway locomotive, the car, the truck, and the airplane. Modern transport has provided personal mobility, and global travel – but at a cost. In busy cities, travel by car can be slower than travel by horse and cart a hundred years ago. Even the skies above us are congested.

Machines need fuel, and burning fuel pollutes the air. The fuel used by most vehicles is made from oil pumped from beneath the ground – oil resources will not last for ever. In future, many of our travels may be restricted. Instead we will explore the electronic super-highways connecting computers around the globe.

 # THE FIRST BOATS

People travelled on water long before they took to wheels on land. The earliest boats were log rafts, animal skins filled with air, or canoes made from reeds or hollowed-out trees. Paddles were in use by 8000 BC. The Inuit kayak and Welsh coracle are both simple, ancient craft. Both use paddles and are light enough to be carried by one person — both are still in use. By about 3000 BC Egyptian sailors had sails as well as paddles, to propel their craft.

► Canoes turn over less easily with an outrigger, an extra float, fastened on one side. The canoe then becomes a twin-hulled catamaran, a design used for thousands of years by islanders in the Pacific.

Prow

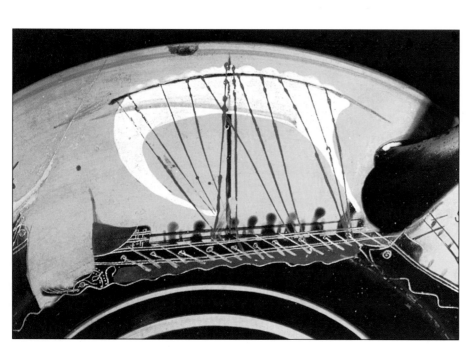

◄ The Ancient Greeks sent ships beyond the Mediterranean, as far north as Britain and the North Sea. They built war galleys with two or three banks of oars for extra power. These warships had an armoured spike or ram in front, to smash into enemy ships. This warship is part of the decoration on a cup made in Athens around 540 BC.

We know from wall paintings in Egyptian tombs that the Egyptians made boats 7,000 years ago. The Egyptians paddled along the River Nile in slender boats made from river reeds, tied in bundles, for timber was scarce. Larger ships had teams of rowers with oars. In 1970, Thor Heyerdahl, a Norwegian anthropologist (1914–) fascinated by ancient seafaring, sailed a replica of an Egyptian reed boat across the Atlantic Ocean.

This demonstration showed that Egyptian sailors could have voyaged at least as far as the island of Crete, and perhaps further.

Later sailors built wooden ships, bigger and stronger. They are called galleys. Like Egyptian ships, they had one large sail, and when there was no wind, or when on a river, they used oars. The galley was steered by a large oar at the stern. In such ships, the Phoenicians (a people who lived in what is now Lebanon) explored and traded as far as the west coast of Africa.

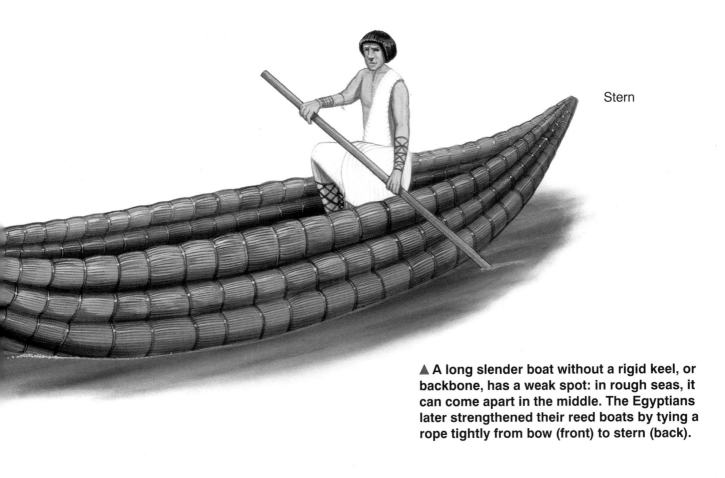

Stern

▲ A long slender boat without a rigid keel, or backbone, has a weak spot: in rough seas, it can come apart in the middle. The Egyptians later strengthened their reed boats by tying a rope tightly from bow (front) to stern (back).

The Romans used large cargo ships to carry grain and wine. They traded with outlying parts of the Roman Empire, such as Britain. Sailors used their knowledge of wind, tides and stars to find their way, but kept close to land as much as possible. Roman cargo ships were up to sixty metres long. It was a thousand years before other European boat builders could surpass them.

CHARIOTS AND CARTS

Imagine a Stone Age farmer about 6,000 years ago clearing a patch of forest. He hacks at a tree with a stone axe. His companions drag away the heavy branches. By chance, a big log falls across two smaller ones. The men push it, and it moves more easily than if it rested on the ground – imagine their surprise, and delight.

The small logs act as rollers, reducing the friction between the big log and the ground. Log rollers made it possible for people to move huge stones, like the ones at Stonehenge, England. Stone Age people also discovered that a load resting on a wooden sled was easier to pull.

Around 3500 BC, Sumerians living in Mesopotamia (in modern Iraq) were the first people to use wheeled carts, pulled by oxen. Their wheels were solid, made from pieces of wood fastened together and rounded to shape. There were no iron tools at that time, and stone tools could not slice tree trunks into neat wheel-shapes. Early wheels often broke as they bumped over rocky tracks.

The wheel was a brilliant idea. It features in most forms of transport, in a whole host of engines, and other mechanical and electrical devices. Probably no other single invention has done more to change the way people live.

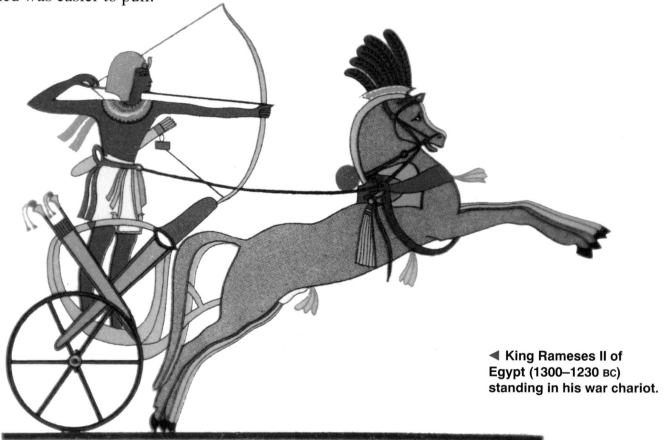

◀ King Rameses II of Egypt (1300–1230 BC) standing in his war chariot.

◀ Wagons pulled by oxen played a vital part in the expansion westward by Europeans across the North American plains. The wagons painted here by the artist Dorenceau are shown crossing the Platte River in Nebraska.

✸ THE FIRST ROAD–BUILDERS

The Romans were the first scientific road-builders. They surveyed routes, using a sighting instrument called a groma. They dug out the ground, and laid a foundation of clay, chalk or gravel. They added cement and a top surface of paving stones. Roman roads were cambered, or angled so that rainwater drained off into ditches at the side. They were also very straight. Some modern roads follow the same routes as Roman roads. After the Romans, road-building in Europe was neglected until the 1800s. A Scottish engineer named John McAdam (1756–1836) built stone-topped roads that vehicles could use in bad weather – unlike dirt roads. The invention of the motor car, with rubber tyres, brought the smooth-topped tarmac or concrete roads of today.

The light, but strong, spoked wheel evolved in Egypt, about 1500 BC. Short, curved sections (now known as felloes) were held together by a tyre made from metal strips nailed to the wood. Spoked wheels were fitted to two-wheeled carts or chariots. Pulled by horses, the chariot was the first war vehicle.

At first, wheel and axle were fixed so that both turned at the same time. Later, the wheel was held on the axle by a pin, so the wheel turned while the axle did not. Soon after 1000 BC four-wheeled carts with a swivelling front axle were being used in southern Europe. They made driving round corners easier, but the idea disappeared and did not resurface until around 1350 in the Middle Ages.

Horses were too valuable to pull carts – that work was left to oxen and donkeys. The horse was a war animal, used in battle by charioteers and cavalry. The essentials of horse harness were the bridle and mouth-bit, saddle, and (invented last, about 200 BC) stirrups. Horses could not pull heavy loads because neck-straps and yokes choked them. About AD 800 the horse-collar solved the problem, and horsepower dominated land transport throughout the Middle Ages.

OCEAN-GOING SHIPS

Transport technology in Europe changed little during the Middle Ages (roughly from AD 500 to 1500). The Vikings sailed their longships across the Atlantic Ocean to Greenland and some even landed in North America, but their ships were no more advanced than the ancient Greek galleys. At that time, the Chinese built the biggest sailing ships in the world. Their sea-going junks had four or five masts, and were steered by a stern rudder (Europeans were still using an extra-large oar). The junk's woven matting sails were easy to operate, and some ships had removable masts. The hull was divided into watertight compartments, so the ship was less likely to sink.

◀ Chinese junks are still built in the traditional way with sails that are easy to adjust.

European ship design began to change in the 1400s. A new design known as a carrack had three masts carrying square and triangular, or lateen, sails. The lateen sail, copied from Mediterranean and Arab ships, was easy to swing to catch the wind. Having both types of sail enabled sailors to adapt to changing wind conditions.

Ships of the 1400s were small. When the Italian-born Christopher Columbus (1451–1506) sailed to America from Spain in 1492, the biggest of his three ships weighed only 80 tonnes. Yet in such small vessels, sailors voyaged not only to America, but also to India (Vasco da Gama, 1498) and around the world (Magellan, 1519–22).

FINDING THE WAY

Out of sight of land, sailors relied on the sun and stars to find their way. The magnetic compass appeared in China by 1100 and in Europe nearly a hundred years later. Medieval sailors used charts known as portolans, based on compass readings. When Christopher Columbus set out westward across the Atlantic Ocean in 1492, he was misled by wildly inaccurate maps. He thought that a few days' sailing would bring his ships to Asia. Instead he landed on islands to the east of a massive continent hitherto unknown to Europeans. During the 1500s, maps improved and sailors could measure the height of the sun above the horizon using instruments known as the astrolabe and the backstaff. From the height of the sun, a navigator could calculate how far the ship was from the equator (its latitude). Estimating position east or west (longitude) was difficult until, in 1761, the English inventor John Harrison (1693–1776) tested the first reliable sea-clock (chronometer) on a voyage to Jamaica.

▲ This Dutch ship painted by the artist Verbbek (1590–1633) is typical of European ships of the sixteenth century.

▼ To find a ship's latitude (distance north or south of the equator), sailors often used an astrolabe. This instrument measured the height of stars from which sailors estimated their position.

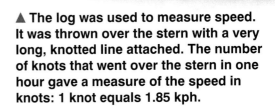

▲ The log was used to measure speed. It was thrown over the stern with a very long, knotted line attached. The number of knots that went over the stern in one hour gave a measure of the speed in knots: 1 knot equals 1.85 kph.

In the 1500s much bigger ships were built. But designing ships was still a craft, not a science. Shipbuilders made drawings, but relied mostly on rough measurements and experience. If a rich person ordered a new ship bigger and more showy than any built before, it was built – even if the result was dangerously top-heavy.

THE STEAM REVOLUTION

Until the 1700s the only way of doing heavy work was by using muscle-power, water or wind. A Greek inventor, Ctesibius of Alexandria, made a pump for water in the second century BC. It used a piston which moved up and down inside a cylinder. Piston pumps worked by hand or animal power were used to pump water from wells and mines right through the Middle Ages. In 1698, an English engineer named Thomas Savery built a steam pump to remove water from flooded mines, but without great success.

Fourteen years later the first proper steam engine was invented. Like Savery's pump, its purpose was to remove unwanted water from mines. The inventor was the English blacksmith, Thomas Newcomen (1663–1729). His engine condensed steam in a cylinder, creating a vacuum, which pulled a piston down. The piston was fixed to one end of a beam, which rocked up and down, like a see-saw. The other end was attached to the piston of the pump in the mine. The engine was reliable and commercially successful, though inefficient. It had no challengers for sixty years.

▼ Symington's steamboat, *Charlotte Dundas* was tested in Scotland during 1801 and 1802. It was intended as a tug boat on the Clyde–Forth Canal but never went into service.

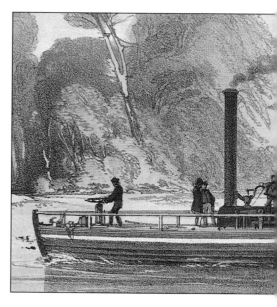

 ## THE CANAL BUILDERS

Canals in Britain had a golden age for a few brief years at the beginning of the Industrial Revolution in the late seventeenth century, when they were the main means of transportation for bulky materials. The canal builders, engineers like Thomas Telford (1757–1834) and James Brindley (1716–1772), were largely self-taught.

The canals fell into disuse because the steam engine was quickly adapted to run on rails and proved a cheaper way of moving freight. The long water routes across Europe, Asia and the USA, however, are still in use today. In the USA, the St Lawrence Seaway links the Atlantic Ocean with Duluth in Minnesota, 3,747 kilometres inland. It was a joint US and Canadian project to build 302 kilometres of canal deep enough to take ocean-going vessels; the project was started in 1954 and the canal opened in 1959.

Lake Erie

Niagara River

Genesee River

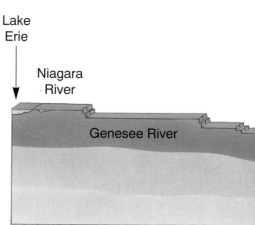

James Watt (1736–1819) was a Scottish engineer who became interested in steam engines after repairing a Newcomen engine when he worked as a technician at Glasgow University. Watt could see ways of making improvements and finally patented his own steam engine in 1759. Further modifications and patents followed, and by 1781 he had an engine that could drive wheels round and round, rather than a beam up and down. The engine had a flywheel, a crank and a spinning 'governor' to control its speed. It was ready to drive the factory machines and vehicles that would enable the Industrial Revolution to take place.

▲ James Watt perfected a steam engine in 1781.

A French engineer named Nicolas Cugnot (1725–1804) made the first steam-driven vehicle in 1769. It moved, slowly, but crashed into a wall and was shut away for everyone's safety. Steam engines performed rather better on water. A steam-driven paddle-boat was made in France in 1783 by the Marquis Jouffroy d'Abbans (1751–1832). In the USA, the inventor John Fitch (1743–1798) built a model steamboat with wheels at the sides in 1785. In 1802 the Scottish engineer, William Symington (1763–1831), completed the first workable steamboat ever built: the *Charlotte Dundas* was intended as a tug to pull barges along the River Forth and the Clyde Canal in Scotland. The first regular steamboat passenger service began in 1807 on the River Hudson in the USA, when the *Clermont* chugged its way from New York to Albany. The steamboat had been built by Robert Fulton (1765–1815), an American engineer. It was so successful that steamers under his patent were used on many US rivers.

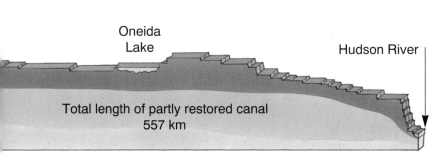

Oneida Lake

Hudson River

Total length of partly restored canal
557 km

◀ The Erie Canal in the United States joins Lake Erie to the Hudson River. Opened in 1825, it covered 580 kilometres and had eighty-three locks. The chief engineer, Benjamin Wright (1770–1842), knew little about canal building at the start of the project but he set high standards and trained his workforce on the job. He became the acknowledged American expert on civil engineering.

THE FIRST RAILWAYS

Speed of travel did not matter much before the 1800s but the Industrial Revolution, the age of factories and machines, changed this. Factories swallowed fuel and raw materials by the wagonloads every day. They poured out goods in unimagined numbers – goods that had to be moved to ports and cities, as fast as possible.

Mineworkers long ago learned that hauling coal trucks was easier if the wheels ran on wooden or iron rails. In 1804 Richard Trevithick (1771–1833), an English mine engineer, took a steam engine from a steam hammer and got it moving on rails. His locomotive pulled a load of ten tonnes at eight kilometres per hour. Trevithick built a steam carriage for passengers, and by 1814, several steam railways were working in collieries in northern England.

▲ Richard Trevithick's steam engine was on trial in London in 1808. Although Trevithick was an ingenious inventor, he was not a very good businessman – he died penniless.

► The Central Pacific Railway was built eastwards across the United States starting from Sacramento in California. Thousands of Chinese labourers were hired to blast out ledges along the steep sides of the Sierra Nevada mountains.

Among the engineers making steam engines were the British inventors, George Stephenson (1781–1848) and his son Robert (1803–1859). In 1825, a locomotive built by the Stephensons travelled from Stockton to Darlington on the world's first public steam railway. The train was made up of wagons and carriages normally pulled by horses. The Stephensons then built an engine called the *Rocket* that won a speed competition to work on the Liverpool to Manchester railway. The first passengers were carried in 1830, amid great excitement, marred by the train fatally injuring one of the officials on the grand opening day.

▼ **The Central Pacific Railroad joined with the Union Pacific on 10 May 1869 at Promontory in Utah. The Union Pacific was built westward from Omaha in Nebraska. The joint railroad was 2,776 kilometres long.**

The speed of railway building was astonishing. Railway fever spread across Europe and the United States, and by 1854 had reached Australia. Locomotives grew bigger and faster. Extra wheels spread the weight of bigger boilers. At first, accidents were all too common. Airbrakes (1869) and signalling systems made train travel safer. Gangs of labourers laid track across mountains and deserts. They bored tunnels, raised embankments, built bridges, dug cuttings. Railways drove into the hearts of cities, to grand new stations – fitting homes for the puffing monsters of steam. For the first time, people could travel faster on land than a horse could gallop. They could send goods by train, go to work by train, and go to the seaside by train. It was a revolution that changed the way people thought about time and distance.

BALLOONS AND AIRSHIPS

On 21 November 1783, amazed Paris citizens watched a yellow and blue taffeta globe rise into the air. From a basketwork gallery below it, two men waved. One was a scientist named Jean de Rozier, the other an aristocrat named the Marquis d'Arlandes. The world's first 'aeronauts' were flying, in a balloon filled with hot air, built by the Montgolfier brothers: Joseph (1740–1810) and Etienne (1745–99). Few in the crowd understood what they saw; to them, it was magic. People had flown toy balloons before, but no one had built one twenty metres high, able to lift two people.

The Montgolfier hot-air balloon was quickly followed into the skies by balloons filled with hydrogen gas. This lighter-than-air gas had been discovered in 1766 by the English scientist, Henry Cavendish (1731–1810). The French physicist, Jacques Charles (1746–1823), flew a hydrogen balloon in France on 1 December 1783. He made the hydrogen by pouring sulphuric acid on to iron filings and water in a barrel. Filling the balloon took four days but the gas balloon soared to 3,000 metres, high enough to give its intrepid pilot a headache.

▲ The Mongolfier balloon rose in the air because a fire below the open mouth of the balloon heated the air inside. The air inside expanded, becoming lighter than the air outside and making the balloon rise up.

▼ The *Hindenburg*, built in 1936, could carry 70 passengers in great luxury. The accommodation was inside the hull and there was even a dance floor. Four large diesel engines produced a speed of almost 140 kilometres per hour.

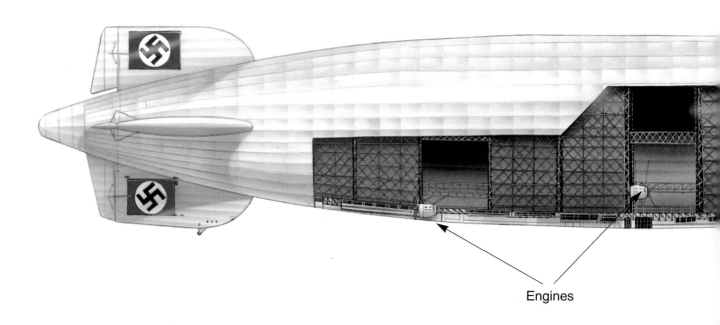

Engines

In the 1800s balloonists made news. They crossed seas and mountains. They did stunts, gave joy-rides and jumped wearing parachutes. They flew above battlefields to spy on the enemy. But balloons go only where the wind blows them, and attempts to steer them with oars or hand-turned propellers proved useless.

In 1852 the French engineer, Henri Giffard, made a cigar-shaped balloon with a steam engine turning a propeller. This was the world's first airship. In 1885 an airship was fitted with one of the new petrol engines. Petrol engines were developed by German engineers, Gottlieb Daimler (1834–1900) and Karl Benz (1844–1929), who were busy building the first motor-cars.

▶ **Modern hot-air balloons drift over the Masai Mara game reserve in Tanzania, Africa. They provide a pleasant and silent means of viewing the countryside.**

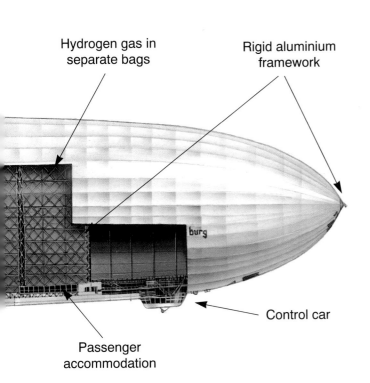

Hydrogen gas in separate bags

Rigid aluminium framework

burg

Control car

Passenger accommodation

During the First World War (1914–18) large German airships, built in a factory started by Count Ferdinand von Zeppelin (1838–1917), dropped bombs on London. By the 1930s passenger airships dwarfing the biggest airplanes were cruising across the Atlantic Ocean. However, the airship had a fatal weakness because hydrogen gas catches fire very easily. When the *Hindenburg* burst into flames on landing at Lakehurst in the USA on 6 May 1937, the future for airships as long-distance transport died with the thirty-five passengers and crew.

Modern airships are used for advertising, pleasure trips and carrying television cameras. They are filled with helium, a gas which cannot burn. Compared to modern airplanes they are slow and difficult to steer.

IRON SHIPS

During the 1800s two important changes took place in ship design. Firstly the large quantities of cheap iron and steel produced by the Industrial Revolution gradually found a use in shipbuilding. Secondly steam engines slowly took over from sails as the best way of powering large ocean-going ships.

At first many of the new steamboats had sails as well as engines, in case they ran out of fuel. They had to be big enough to carry enough coal or wood to keep their boilers working between ports, particularly if they were crossing the Atlantic Ocean. They also had paddle-wheels, but these large wheels were not very efficient and sometimes broke in rough seas. In 1843 a British engineer, Isambard Kingdom Brunel (1806–1859), launched the *Great Britain*, the first large ship to be constructed from iron. She was ninety-eight metres long, weighed 3,300 tonnes and had a propeller instead of paddle-wheels, making her the forerunner of all modern ships.

In 1750, the Swiss-born mathematician, Daniel Bernoulli (1700–1782), had suggested that steamboats could be driven by the kind of screw used in the ancient world as a water pump. To work well, it had to be turned quickly by a powerful engine, and it was not until 1836 that the English inventor, Francis Smith (1808–1874), fitted an Archimedean screw to a boat. The screw broke during tests leaving a stump that was very similar to modern propellers – it also made the boat go much faster!

▲ Francis Smith built the screw steamboat, HMS *Rattler*, for the British navy in 1843. On 3 April 1845, *Rattler* won a tug of war with the paddle-driven sister-ship HMS *Alecto*, proving for all time that propellers are much better than paddles.

▶ The *Lusitania* carried passengers across the Atlantic Ocean between Liverpool in Britain and New York, USA. This luxury liner had giant turbine engines, giving it a top speed of 25 knots.

In 1884 the English engineer, Charles Parsons (1854–1931), invented a new kind of high-speed steam engine – the steam turbine – and in 1894 he fitted one of these engines to a small boat called *Turbinia*. With a top speed of nearly sixty-five kilometres per hour it was faster than any other ship afloat. He showed its paces by making an unofficial visit to a review of the British navy at Spithead in 1897, and sailing rings round the naval patrol boat sent out to intercept it. The navy ordered the turbine-engine ship HMS *Viper* as a result, and in 1907 steam turbines were installed in the *Lusitania* and the *Mauretania*. By 1939, there were more than 80 giant passenger liners in service.

 ## BRUNEL: GENIUS ENGINEER

Isambard Kingdom Brunel (1806–59) was born in England, the son of a French-born civil engineer. He designed the Clifton Suspension Bridge near Bristol, and in 1833 became chief engineer of the Great Western Railway.

Brunel is mostly remembered for his three great steamships: firstly the *Great Western* (1837) which was built to take passengers from the Great Western Railway across the Atlantic Ocean to America, and then the *Great Britain* (1843). Finally, in 1858 after many problems, he saw the enormous *Great Eastern* slide into the water. This monster was 19,000 tonnes, 211 metres long and had a double skin of iron. Built with a screw, paddle-wheels and sails, the *Great Eastern* was intended to carry 4,000 passengers to Australia, but proved a commercial disaster because the engines burned twice as much coal as Brunel had calculated. The ship made history by laying the first transatlantic telegraph cable, and remained the largest ship afloat until scrapped in 1889. Worn out by overwork, Brunel died of a stroke soon after the *Great Eastern*'s first sea trip.

THE BICYCLE

No one seems to have taken two-wheel transport seriously before the early 1800s, when push-along bicycles, known as 'poor man's horses' or hobbyhorses, became popular. Baron Drais von Sauerbron invented a 'running machine' in Germany in 1817. He pushed it along with his feet, but had difficulty turning corners. Denis Johnson in Britain then made a better version, known as a pedestrian curricle. This was made of lighter materials and had improved steering. It was four times as fast as walking, and 'dandyhorses' became fashionable exercise machines. The Baron made nothing from his invention and died penniless.

▲ The penny farthing was difficult to mount and some cyclists used steps to reach the saddle. In 1878 the *Scientific American* stated that the penny farthing was 'an ever-saddled horse that eats nothing and requires no care'.

In 1839 Kirkpatrick Macmillan, a Scottish blacksmith, made a bicycle driven by foot-treadles, but the backwards and forwards movement was awkward and tiring. Philip Fischer's crankpedals of the 1850s were much easier on the legs. His design was copied by Ernest Michaux, a French coach-builder, who started the first bicycle factory in the 1860s.

Bicycles could be made cheaply in factories. The first bicycles were real 'boneshakers', with wooden wheels. Women as well as men took to cycling with enthusiasm. In 1870, James Starley (1831–1881), an English inventor, designed the first penny farthing and his nephew, John Starley, built the first Rover safety cycle in 1885.

Bicycle riding became much smoother in 1888 when John Boyd Dunlop (1840–1921), a Scottish veterinary surgeon, invented air-filled rubber tyres for his son's tricycle wheels. A racing cyclist asked for similar wheels, Dunlop opened a factory, and the 'pneumatic tyre' took its place in history.

◀ The use of bicycles became official policy in China where an estimated 77 million people pedalled to work in the 1980s.

The bicycle is still a cheap ride and healthy exercise, and there are many millions of cyclists worldwide. The latest high-tech racing bikes have streamlined carbon-fibre bodies, disc wheels (fixed to blades instead of forks), and steering columns instead of handlebars. There are miniature bikes, folding bikes and mountain bikes. The bicycle is a design that works, and will go on working as long as people enjoy pedalling.

▼ This advanced racing bike has revolutionary low steering, a three-spoked front wheel fastened to a single blade, and a rear disc wheel.

THE PETROL-ENGINED CAR

Road vehicles with steam engines were tried out during the 1800s but they were heavy, needed coal and water and sometimes blew up. The motor-car came about as a result of a series of inventions made between 1860 and 1885. The first was a gas engine, built in 1860 by the French inventor, Etienne Lenoir (1822–1900). This was a stationary piston engine, burning coal gas, used to drive machinery in factories. Nikolaus Otto, a German engineer (1832–1891), developed a more powerful four-stroke gas engine in 1876.

During this time a new fuel became available. Petroleum oil from the USA was refined to make oils suitable for paraffin lamps and to lubricate factory machines. Petroleum spirit, or petrol, was left over from the refining process. A number of engineers, including Otto experimented with building engines that used petrol.

The German engineer, Gottlieb Daimler (1834–1900), had visited Lenoir's factory in 1860 and later worked for Nikolaus Otto developing new engines. In 1882 Daimler left the Otto factory to concentrate on building his own petrol engine. The first Daimler experimental car was built in 1886, but was really a horseless carriage fitted with a petrol engine. It had a top speed of about fourteen kilometres per hour. Unknown to Daimler, a near-neighbour named Karl Benz (1844–1929), was about to make history.

▼ An early Benz four-wheeled car. It has simple lever steering, and spoked cart-type wheels. There is no protection for the passengers against bad weather.

Steering tiller

Internal combustion engine mounted at the rear on early cars

Diffferential gear allowing back wheels to turn at different speeds when cornering

BERTA BENZ

Karl Benz had an able partner in his wife Berta. She helped in the design of his car, and encouraged him to go on testing it at night, after the commotion its daytime appearances created led to police complaints. Berta pedalled away on her sewing machine to drive a generator to recharge the battery. In 1888, she drove the car on its first cross-country trip. She had to buy petrol from a chemist's shop and used one of her garters as insulating tape to repair an electrical fault. Her day-long trip proved that the car worked. There were many hurdles still to be overcome – including money, for at first few people were willing to buy a Benz car, or indeed any 'horseless carriage'. But the Benzes persisted, interest slowly grew, and in 1893 they exhibited a Benz car in Chicago, USA.

▲ Karl Benz in 1925, aged eighty-one, sitting in the first car he ever built.

Gear stick

Centre point steering allowing the front axle to swivel

Solid rubber tyres

Karl Benz started a business making gas engines for factories in 1879. Building a car was a hobby that became an obsession. He assembled all the parts – carburettor, electrical ignition, and steering (a lever to the front wheels). A large flywheel was spun to start the engine. The flywheel kept spinning to store power so that the engine kept running throughout the four-stroke cycle. He borrowed ideas from the bicycle to provide wheels and gears, and designed a water cooling system for the engine. On 29 January 1886 Karl Benz was awarded a patent for the Patent Motor Car. By 1900, 4,000 three-gear 'Comfortable' models had been sold, and the Benz company was the largest automobile manufacturer in Europe.

☀ INTO THE AIR

▲ On 17 December 1903, *Flyer* took to the air for the first time.

From earliest times people dreamed of flying like birds. Some would-be fliers leaped from towers wearing wings. Flapping feebly, they crashed to earth. Yet, while these brave but misguided experiments went on, a practical flying machine was soaring at the end of a line – the kite. The Chinese and Koreans flew kites for fun, probably as early as 1000 BC. In 1752 the American statesman and scientist, Benjamin Franklin (1706–1790), flew a kite into a thunderstorm, to investigate the nature of lightning.

The kite in flight is subject to the same forces as an airplane. The string tugs it forwards (thrust), the wind pushes it upwards (lift). Yet no scientist studied kite flying seriously until in 1799 the English inventor, George Cayley (1773–1857), began designing model gliders – basically a winged kite without a string. Cayley worked out a practical theory of flight in a heavier-than-air machine. In 1853, he even sent his reluctant coachman, John Appleby, aloft in a glider. Enthusiasts such as the German engineer, Otto Lilienthal (1848–1896), soared many times off hillsides showing that a person could fly with fixed wings for a short distance – he died in a gliding accident.

◀ France was the first country to establish an aircraft industry. This poster advertised an air show at Rheims in 1909.

24

Various inventors designed fanciful steam-airplanes, but steam engines were far too heavy for flight. The lighter petrol engine offered a new opportunity. In the USA and Europe, inventors began experimenting with powered gliders. Among them were the American brothers, Orville (1871–1948) and Wilbur Wright (1867–1912).

On 17 December 1903 the Wrights took their *Flyer* to a lonely stretch of sandhills in North Carolina. Orville lay down at the controls, the propeller whirled, and the flimsy machine lifted into the air. It flew 37 metres. Only five people saw the history-making triumph. The Wrights went on to make much longer flights, but it was some time before the outside world learned of their achievements. In 1905 they offered their invention to the US government, and in 1909 the US army bought its first airplane.

 # THE WRIGHT WAY

Orville and Wilbur Wright lived in Dayton, Ohio in the USA. Neither went to university or studied engineering. As boys they built a toy helicopter, powered by an elastic band, and made kites. They worked together as adults, first as printers and then running a bicycle shop. In their spare time they built gliders.

The Wright brothers were very methodical. They read reports about the experiences of pioneer glider pilots, like Lilienthal, and they built a wind tunnel, to test different wing shapes for their own gliders. Once satisfied, they designed a powered airplane. They built propellers and an engine, and also designed a system for controlling the plane in the air – by twisting or 'warping' the wings. Their successful flight in 1903 did not make newspaper headlines, but by 1912 the Wrights were famous, selling their airplanes in Europe as well as in the USA. Wilbur died of typhoid fever in 1912. Orville sold the business, and died in 1948.

In 1914, airplanes went to war. The First World War (1914–18) speeded up air technology dramatically. By 1918 planes could fly at 240 kilometres per hour, there were four-engined planes, and the British air force alone had 22,000 aircraft. In 1919 the Atlantic Ocean was crossed by a plane for the first time, and regular passenger services soon followed. In less than twenty years after the Wrights' flight, aviation had made an amazing technological leap forward.

SUBMARINES

A number of brave inventors experimented with undersea boats before the submarine became a realistic fighting ship. In 1620 the Dutchman, Cornelis van Drebbel, working in England for King James I, managed to cross the River Thames in England with a primitive submarine made of greased leather stretched over a wooden frame. Not surprisingly it leaked! A one-man submarine called *Turtle* was designed by the American engineer, David Bushnell, in 1776 and used in an unsuccessful attack on the British warship *Eagle,* in New York harbour, during the War of American Independence (1775–1783).

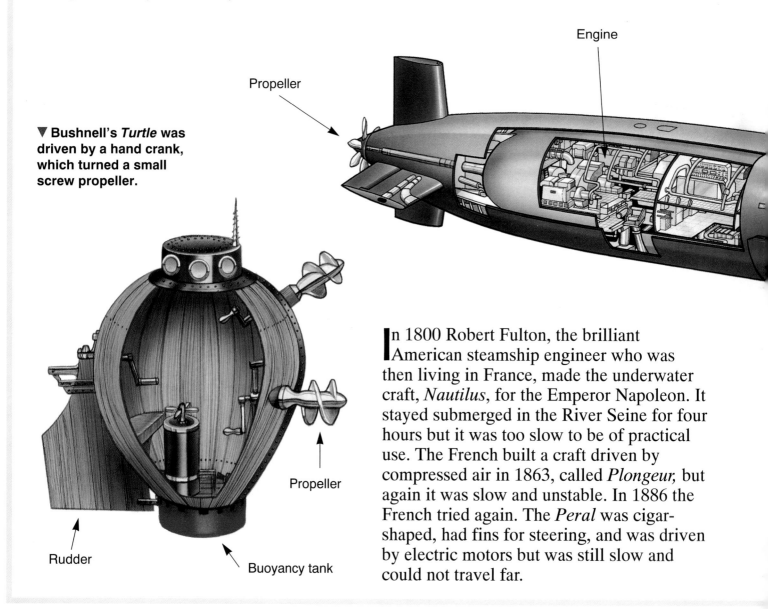

▼ Bushnell's *Turtle* was driven by a hand crank, which turned a small screw propeller.

Engine

Propeller

Propeller

Rudder

Buoyancy tank

In 1800 Robert Fulton, the brilliant American steamship engineer who was then living in France, made the underwater craft, *Nautilus*, for the Emperor Napoleon. It stayed submerged in the River Seine for four hours but it was too slow to be of practical use. The French built a craft driven by compressed air in 1863, called *Plongeur,* but again it was slow and unstable. In 1886 the French tried again. The *Peral* was cigar-shaped, had fins for steering, and was driven by electric motors but was still slow and could not travel far.

Finally in 1900, the Irish-born American, John P. Holland (1841–1914), successfully showed *Holland VI* to the US navy on and under the Potomac River. It had a range of 800 kilometres on the surface and thirty-eight kilometres underwater. It could fire torpedoes large enough to sink a battleship and had a periscope that could be raised to view the scene above the water. Here was a fighting machine to interest the navies of the world.

During the First World War submarines sank many cargo ships as well as warships. During the Second World War (1939-1945) the balance in the deadly undersea war first favoured the German submarines or U-boats, but with the development of sonar (echo-detection) and radar, the advantage tilted towards the hunters on the surface – ships and aircraft.

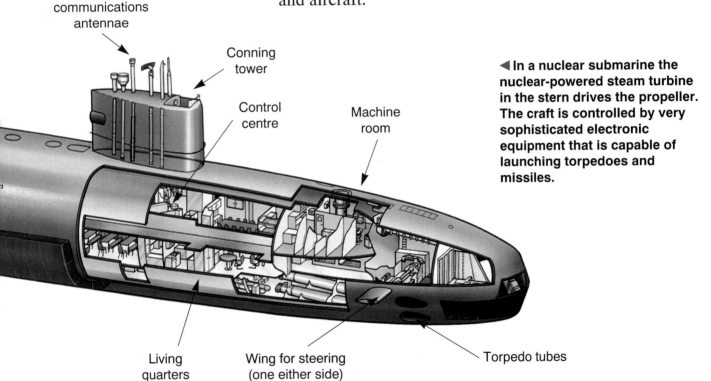

Periscope and communications antennae

Conning tower

Control centre

Machine room

◀ In a nuclear submarine the nuclear-powered steam turbine in the stern drives the propeller. The craft is controlled by very sophisticated electronic equipment that is capable of launching torpedoes and missiles.

Living quarters

Wing for steering (one either side)

Torpedo tubes

In 1954 the US navy launched *Nautilus,* the world's first nuclear submarine. Today, nuclear submarines are the most powerful naval warships. They can be very big (weighing up to 20,000 tonnes) and are whale-shaped, to reduce water resistance. The nuclear reactor heats steam to drive turbine engines, and underwater a nuclear submarine can travel as fast as most surface ships. Sucking in air through snorkel tubes, it can circle the world without surfacing.

THE ROAD REVOLUTION

Many people were suspicious of motor-cars when they were first invented. In Britain, the 'red flag' law of 1865 forced all self propelled-vehicles to crawl behind a walker with a red flag. In France people were more sympathetic and racing on public highways became accepted. This gave French manufacturers a great advantage because they could test cars at speed. French inventors such as Emile Levassor made cars more comfortable, with covered roofs and from 1895 air-filled tyres. Levassor moved the engine to the front of the car, and made other mechanical improvements. By 1900 all the main features of the motor-car had been developed.

▼ **Today Henry Ford's Model T is highly prized by people who collect vintage cars.**

In both Europe and the United States cars were hand-built to order and therefore expensive. Only rich people could afford them, but in the United States the numbers of cars began to increase, despite the high price. In 1902 there was one car for every one and a half million US citizens. By 1907 there was one for every eight hundred. Henry Ford (1863–1947) had been making cars in Detroit since 1903. He was convinced cars could be made cheaper and in October 1908 he launched his Model T – the immortal 'Tin Lizzie'. The Model T was very basic, strong and light. It was built for inexperienced drivers and rough roads, and cost less than half the price of other cars. It was made from standard parts, and by the summer of 1913, he had devised a production line with 2,000 cars a month rolling off.

☀ **HENRY FORD**

Henry Ford was born on a farm in Michigan, USA. He left school when he was fifteen to work as a apprentice in a machine shop. He built his first car in 1893 when he was thirty years old. It was the only car in Detroit and Ford drove it for 1,600 kilometres before selling it.

He was employed by the local electric power company who offered him promotion if he would stop tinkering with his 'gas buggies'. Instead he left his job in 1899 to form his own company in Detroit and later the Ford Motor Company in 1903. After a number of years of experiment and struggle he finally built the Model T in 1908. In the first year, with $100,000 of capital, 10,607 cars were built. By 1927 there were more than 15 million Model Ts on the road and the company had $700 million in reserve.

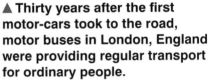

▲ **Thirty years after the first motor-cars took to the road, motor buses in London, England were providing regular transport for ordinary people.**

▶ **Modern motorways, like this one in Spessart, Germany, allow people to reach places that were not easily accessible fifty years ago.**

Gradually the roads improved to keep pace with the increasing numbers of vehicles. Motor buses, electric trams and trolley-buses provided public transport for people without cars – still the majority in industrialized countries before the Second World War. In the 1920s and 1930s the first super-highways for fast cars and trucks were built in Germany and Italy. During the 1950s car ownership increased rapidly, particularly in Europe and North America. Motorways now criss-cross many countries of the world. The car has changed old cities, created new suburbs and altered the way people live.

Today the emphasis in new car design is on safety, and the production line is operated by robots. In 1909 the French chemist, Edouard Benedictus, sandwiched celluloid between two sheets of glass to make safety glass. Today many car windscreens are made of glass laminated with plastic, seat belts are compulsory, steering wheels collapse on impact and airbags inflate to protect drivers. Car bodies are designed to crumple and absorb the energy of impact.

ELECTRIC AND DIESEL TRAINS

In 1879 the German inventor, Werner von Siemens (1816–1892), showed a small electric locomotive at the Berlin Trades Exhibition, and in 1881 a Berlin tramway was run on electricity. The Volks Electric Railway opened along Brighton beach, southern England, in 1883 and in the same year the Giant's Causeway and Portrush Railway opened in Northern Ireland. Other little electric railways swiftly started up across Europe and the USA. The Baltimore and Ohio Railroad in the USA opened the world's first main line electric railway through a tunnel under the city of Baltimore in 1895.

Electric locomotives were lighter, cleaner, and more efficient than steam engines, but the main problems were the method of supplying the electricity to the trains and the high voltages involved in transmitting the current efficiently along the railway lines. European railways were quick to develop electrification for long distance travel while Britain clung to steam.

◀ A train heads out of Paris, France, on its way to the Channel Tunnel. Specially-built for the Paris–London run, Channel Tunnel trains can run on both British and French track.

The diesel engine was invented in 1897 by Rudolf Diesel, a German engineer (1858–1913). He designed an engine without spark plugs which burned cheap oil instead of the more expensive petrol. It was shown at an exhibition in Munich in 1898 and its inventor soon became a millionaire. The first diesel railway locomotive ran in 1912 on the Prussian–Hessian State Railway in Germany, and by 1934 massive diesel locomotives were hauling freight and passenger trains across the USA.

By the 1950s, diesel and electric trains were shunting steam off the main lines and into history. No steam train ever ran faster than 201.16 kilometres per hour – a record set by the *Mallard* in Britain in 1938. The French TGV electric express trains daily produce an average speed of just over 212 kilometres per hour on the Paris–Lyon run, and these super-fast expresses now compete with airlines on the main inter-city routes in Europe.

Today, railways run diesel or electric trains though in some parts of the world steam still survives. The decision as to which type of power to use is based on the cost of installation, the length of the journey, the number of passengers travelling and the competition provided by other means of transport.

▲ **A powerful diesel locomotive moves freight through a train yard in Oregon, USA.**

☀ UNDERGROUND RAILWAYS

To solve the problem of building railways in crowded cities, nineteenth-century engineers went underground. The first underground railway was London's Metropolitan Railway, completed in 1863. Its tunnels were trenches covered over, rather than deep tunnels. Steam and smoke from the steam locomotives filled the tunnels and enveloped passengers waiting on stations. The locomotives were fitted with 'smoke-eating' devices, which did not really work. In 1890 the City and South London Railway was the first real 'tube' railway. It used electric trains, putting an end to the smoky tunnels.

The track circuit system, automatically controlling signals on sections of track, was invented in the USA in 1872, and ensured that trains on the same line but only a minute or so apart did not collide. Modern underground railways are almost completely automated. Passengers can buy tickets from a machine; electronic gates 'read' the ticket; trains run by remote-control along computer-monitored tracks. But passengers still like to see a driver, and staff on the platform.

CIVIL AIRCRAFT

In the 1920s aircraft engineers realized that if an aircraft had a streamlined shape, it would have a greater speed because there would be less drag from the air. By 1935 aircraft had become all-metal monoplanes with several propellers and an undercarriage that tucked inside the plane during flight. They were fast and comfortable and delivered passengers, mail and other cargo around the world.

The jet engine was a development of the gas turbine engine and it made planes go even faster. In the 1930s two young engineers, Frank Whittle (1907–) in Britain and Pabst von Ohain (1911–) in Germany, working separately, produced jet engines that did not need propellers. Ohain fitted his new engine into a Heinkel HE 178 and the first jet plane took to the air on 27 August 1939, though it was not a particularly inspiring aircraft. Whittle's turbo-jet engine was far more impressive. On 15 May 1941 a Gloster E28/39 took off and achieved a top speed of 544 kilometres per hour. When fitted with a more powerful turbo-jet the Gloster managed 705 kilometres per hour. As tests continued they proved that jet engines worked even better at higher speeds and greater altitudes.

▲ A Gloster E28/39 fitted with an early version of the jet engine.

◀ Concorde on the tarmac at Britain's Heathrow Airport, London, with a Boeing 747 jumbo jet behind.

After the Second World War, the USA, the USSR, Britain and France competed to build faster and bigger jet planes. In 1957 about 90 million people travelled on the world's airlines. When the US Boeing company launched the Boeing 707 in 1958, it was quickly followed by a whole family of Boeing planes. During the 1960s the air travel industry developed rapidly worldwide, and by 1971 Boeing designs accounted for 2,200 of the 3,600 jet airliners then in service. The massive Boeing 747 entered service in January 1970. With its turbofan engines it was quieter than previous jets and its huge capacity – up to 490 passengers – made it very cost-effective.

The supersonic Anglo–French Concorde went into service in 1976, transporting up to 100 passengers across the Atlantic Ocean in about three hours – most of the time at twice the speed of sound. Technically advanced in its day, but very expensive, Concorde was not a sales success. Airlines preferred bigger if slower passenger carriers, like the Boeing 747 and European Airbus.

By 1979, sixty years after the first daily passenger services, 750 million air tickets a year were being sold.

 ## GLAMOROUS GLENNIS

On 14 October 1947 in California, USA, the rocket-powered Bell XS-1 flew faster than the speed of sound. The plane was flown by Captain Chuck Yeager and named *Glamorous Glennis* after his wife.

As a plane approaches the speed of sound (about 1,125 kilometres an hour) it passes through a shock wave, and there is a loud bang known as the sonic boom. Some experts believed the aircraft would be destroyed by the shock, but the fear proved to be without foundation. It was then only a matter of time before aircraft were designed to carry passengers at supersonic speed.

HELICOPTERS

The Italian artistic genius, Leonardo da Vinci (1452–1519), sketched designs in his notebook for a machine similar to a helicopter. It had a screw-like spinning rotor made from iron wire and cloth. As a child he may have played with a 'Chinese top', a flying toy with feather rotors which had been known for at least 2,000 years before it reached Europe in the Middle Ages. Leonardo's machine would probably have flown had there been an engine to supply the power needed to turn the screw, but a suitable engine was about 350 years in the future.

▲ The helicopter is ideal for air-sea rescue, because of its ability to hover over a ship, lower rescuers, and lift off people in danger.

▲ Igor Sikorsky at the controls of his VS-300 helicopter on 14 September 1939.

The first helicopter to fly steadily and well was built by Heinrich Focke of Germany in 1936. It had twin rotor blades set on outriggers. In 1939 Igor Sikorsky (1889–1972), a Russian engineer working in the USA, designed a helicopter with just one rotor blade. He worked out that if the rotor blades could be tilted to 'bite' into the air, a pilot could make the helicopter fly forwards, backwards or sideways. To stop the whole aircraft spinning in one direction as the rotor turned in the other (this twisting force is called torque), a second smaller rotor on the tail spun vertically. This countered the torque, and also helped steer the helicopter. In 1942 an improved version of the VS-300 helicopter, the R-4, went into production. All modern single-rotor helicopters are based on this design.

▲ A Bell-Boeing V22 Osprey photographed in June 1993. The Osprey is a tilt-rotor design. It flies more like a fixed-wing airplane, but does not need a long runway.

Since those early days, helicopters have got bigger, flown faster and become indispensable. The first air-sea rescue by helicopter was in 1945 off Long Island, New York in the USA, when two men stranded on a wrecked tanker in a gale were winched off after sixteen hours. Adopted by armies and navies around the world to support troops and hunt for submarines, helicopters also have a multitude of commercial uses from supplying oil rigs to finding shipping lanes through ice fields. As flying cranes they perform jobs that would otherwise be extremely difficult – in 1962 it was an RAF helicopter that placed the cross on top of the new Coventry Cathedral in England.

For passenger transport, helicopters are noisy and use too much fuel but there is no doubt about their advantage over fixed-wing aircraft. Only the Harrier jump jet, using swivelling nozzles to direct the jet thrust from its engines, can match the helicopter for manoeuvrability. Tilt-wing aircraft, which take off like a helicopter and then tilt their wings (and engines) to fly forwards at speed, would be assured of a future – if they could be made to fly quietly.

☀ BIG LOADERS

The more goods that can be moved on one vehicle, the cheaper the transport cost per item. This simple piece of economics has caused engineers to build bigger – bigger trucks, bigger planes, bigger ships. Brunel's *Great Eastern* at 19,000 tonnes was too big for 1858 – it was out of step with the technology of its time. By the 1900s, the world was ready for mass transport, and in 1930s shipyards were launching passenger liners of 40,000 tonnes and upwards that remained economic until passenger jet aircraft swept them aside in the 1960s. The *Queen Mary,* at 81,237 tonnes, was launched in 1934 and taken out of service thirty three years later. The ship could carry 2,000 passengers.

▶ Natural gas is carried in huge refrigerated tankers. At −162°C the gas is liquid but some does evaporate into the air space inside the tanks. This gas can be siphoned off and used as a boiler fuel for the ship.

The first modern-style oil tanker was the *Gluckauf,* built in 1886 at 3,000 tonnes. It was a dwarf compared to the *Hellas Fos,* the largest tanker and ship of any kind in service a hundred years later. The *Hellas Fos,* weighing 555,051 tonnes, is a steam turbine tanker built in 1979. Since the 1950s, oil fuel has been in huge demand for cars and power stations. This has encouraged shippers to built giant tankers. Before the 1950s cargo ships were smaller than passenger ships. Few were over 40,000 tonnes. Huge tankers are too large to pass through the Suez or Panama canals, but they carry enormous cargoes, and the cost-savings compensate for longer journey times. Ships carrying bulk cargoes like natural gas and metal ores can be as large as 350,000 tonnes, like the *Berge Stahl* which was launched at Ulsan, South Korea in 1986.

Costs are also reduced if less time is spent loading and unloading the cargo. In 1955 the tanker *Ideal X* was converted to carry containers on her decks. Today purpose-built container ships transport manufactured goods around the world, spending a minimum of time in port. At a container port, such as the Rotterdam-Europoort in the Netherlands, the containers arrive on trucks. They are lifted off by cranes and piled up in computer-controlled waiting areas alongside the docks. When a container ship comes into port, one load of containers can be quickly replaced by another.

◀ A container arrives by truck at the modern docks in Baltimore, USA. In the background a container ship is being loaded.

In 1900 most overland freight was carried by the railways. Freight began to transfer from the railways to trucks in the 1920s, after the First World War had boosted truck production and brought improvements in truck size and reliability. After the 1950s the new, faster motorways were soon filled by new and bigger trucks, some weighing fifty tonnes when fully loaded. Specialized trucks can be gigantic: the world's biggest dumper truck has a loaded weight of 549 tonnes. Many trucks are built to carry containers to and from the ports. The engine and driver's cab form a detachable 'tractor' unit, hitched to a trailer on which containers are carried. Most big trucks have diesel engines, and are fitted with streamlined wind deflectors to cut air resistance, and so save fuel, and money.

ROCKETS AND SPACECRAFT

▲ On 12 April 1961, Russian astronaut, Yuri Gagarin, became the first person to travel in space. A giant rocket put his spacecraft, Vostok 1, into orbit around the Earth. The flight lasted 108 minutes. He made one complete circuit of the Earth and landed safely less than ten kilometres from the calculated point.

Rockets were used by the Chinese about 2,000 years ago as fireworks or weapons, and rockets were in use in Europe by the 1300s. A rocket is a cylinder packed with fuel. When the fuel burns, gases rush out of the bottom propelling the cylinder high into the air. During the 1800s science-fiction writers imagined people flying into space, either fired from cannon as in Jules Verne's book *From the Earth to the Moon* (1873) or inside rockets. Scientists were much more sceptical. Many dismissed spaceflight as impossible. A Russian teacher, Konstantin Tsiolkovski (1857–1935), wrote out the theory of space-rocket flight in 1903. His work inspired physicists, like Robert Goddard (1882–1945) in the USA, and by 1926 Goddard successfully launched his first rocket from a desert in New Mexico, USA.

The first long-range rocket, the V2, was built as a bomb-carrying weapon during the Second World War by German engineer Werner von Braun (1912–1977). It had a range of about 320 kilometres, rose 96 kilometres in the air and descended at several times the speed of sound. After the war, captured V2s and German scientists were taken to the USA and the USSR. In 1957 a powerful Russian rocket put the first artificial satellite, Sputnik 1, into orbit around the Earth, and in April 1961 carried Yuri Gagarin, the first person to fly in space, into orbit.

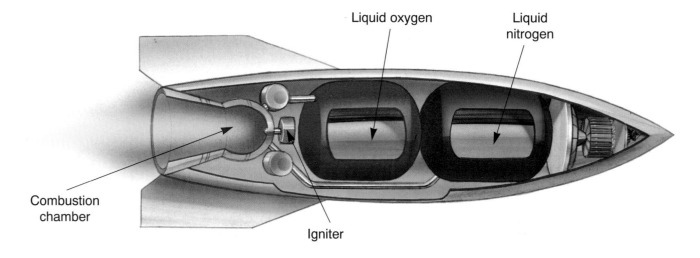

Liquid oxygen

Liquid nitrogen

Combustion chamber

Igniter

International prestige then fuelled the space race. The US President, John F. Kennedy (1917–1963), announced the Apollo space programme, which aimed to put an American on the moon by the end of the 1960s. Huge sums of money were spent. In July 1969 a Saturn V rocket, designed by von Braun's team, launched Apollo 11, and the American astronauts, Neil Armstrong and Edwin Aldrin, became the first human beings to set foot on the moon. Since then ten other astronauts have visited the moon – all of them Americans.

Multi-stage rockets, like Saturn V, can only be used once, as most of the rocket is destroyed during the escape from the Earth's gravity. The first of the space shuttle fleet, *Columbia*, was launched from Cape Kennedy, USA, in 1981. Space shuttles are a combination of rocket, space station and glider and are still the world's only reusable spacecraft. In 1986 the USSR launched the Mir space station. It is an orbiting laboratory visited regularly by teams of astronauts, some of whom have spent more than a year in orbit. In June 1995 space shuttle *Atlantis* made a significant advance, by successfully docking with the Mir space station. A new international space station is planned, to continue research into human flight.

▲ Space shuttle *Columbia* climbs away from the launch pad on 5 June 1991. A shuttle travels into space strapped to a huge fuel tank and driven by two powerful booster rockets. First the booster rockets and then the fuel tank fall away before the shuttle reaches orbit. When returning to Earth the shuttle makes a controlled landing on a runway like a glider.

◄ Many rockets use liquid nitrogen as a fuel. This is mixed with liquid oxygen in the combustion chamber where the nitrogen ignites explosively. As gases rush out of the exhaust the rocket is propelled forwards with an equal and opposite force.

The space programmes have spawned a vast space industry. Factories build communications, weather, spy and navigation satellites. They also provide spacecraft, rocket engines, computers, spacesuits, special space foods, and life support systems for astronauts working in space. However, although robotic space probes have been sent to all of the planets in the solar system, with the exception of Pluto, extensive space travel by human beings still remains highly unlikely at the present time.

ALTERNATIVE TRANSPORT

Inventions made in the last 200 years – railways, cars, airplanes – have enabled people to move further and faster than ever before. Yet the telecommunications revolution of the last ten years may, in future, make many journeys unnecessary. More people may work from home, shop by telephone, communicate globally via Internet and video telephone. But goods will still have to be manufactured and raw materials, goods and people will still have to be moved around the world.

▲ One of the six natural-gas-powered buses which in 1995 were undergoing trials at Trondheim in Norway.

Science, technology, need, money and governments will shape the transport systems of the next century. We need cleaner, more efficient vehicles, to reduce pollution and environmental damage. We need to conserve the Earth's resources and develop new alternative sources of energy to preserve the Earth's precious stocks of oil, gas and coal. We once hoped that nuclear power would provide limitless energy, but it is neither limitless, cheap nor risk-free. We are beginning to make better use of wind power, ocean tides, and the heat of the sun. We still need to waste less and preserve more.

▼ The hydrofoil is not a new invention. The first commercial hydrofoil went into service in 1956, between Sicily and the Italian mainland. Because the craft rides mostly above the water, friction is reduced, allowing it to move faster. However, the foils damage easily and as the weight of the craft increases, the power required to drive it at speed increases dramatically.

▲ At the Frankfurt Motor Show in 1991, BMW exhibited its electric car, the BMW E1. Electric cars have limited range and power because they are battery-driven. Electric cars are not new. Manufacturers have been experimenting with them for thirty years. The problem is the batteries: they need to be light, long-lasting and easily rechargeable.

The car is a worldwide symbol of status and personal mobility. Car manufacture is a huge industry that provides many people with a living. Yet motor vehicles cause much of the congestion and pollution that invade our large cities and motorway networks. Electric cars are much quieter and cleaner but they cannot travel far or fast, or move heavy loads. To protect our well-being, we need to both change the way we live and clean up the exhaust gases produced by our transport. We need to provide as much personal mobility and freedom as possible, and effective ways of moving goods and people around the world.

TIMELINE OF ADVANCE

Here are some of the people, discoveries, inventions and improvements that have helped shape the transport we use today.

Middle East, Egypt, China The wheel (inventor unknown) came into being in about 3500 BC, before the cart or the tame horse. Domestic animals such as asses, oxen, camels and dogs were used to carry and drag loads long before then.

Mediterranean About 3000 BC Egyptian, and later Phoenician and Greek, sailors ventured to sea in sailing ships to explore and trade.

Ancient Romans From the first century AD the Romans built stone-topped roads across their empire mainly for the army but also for trade. Roman cargo ships were the largest of their time, matched only by Chinese junks.

Ancient Chinese By about AD 1100 the Chinese had built canals, invented the kite, the gunpowder rocket and the magnetic compass.

Leonardo da Vinci An Italian artist and inventor (1452–1519) who sketched various machines including a helicopter and an armoured fighting vehicle – none of which were ever built.

▲ Robert Fulton.

Isaac Newton A British scientist (1642–1727) who worked out a theory of gravitation and described the three laws of force and motion, published in his book *Philosophie Naturalis Principia Mathematica* in 1687.

James Watt A Scottish engineer (1736–1819) who improved the steam engine, making it more powerful, and converted its motion from vertical to rotary.

Joseph Montgolfier A French paper-maker (1740–1810) who with his brother **Etienne** (1745–1799) built the first hot-air balloon to fly with human passengers in 1783.

Richard Trevithick An English engineer (1781–1833) who built steam-engined vehicles for road and rail, proving that steam was a new power source for transport.

George Stephenson A British engineer (1781–1848) who designed the locomotive for the world's first passenger steam railway. His son **Robert** (1803–1859) was also a railway engineer.

Robert Fulton An American inventor (1756–1815) who built a submarine in 1800, and also the steamboat *Clermont,* which ran the first public steamboat service in 1807.

George Cayley A British scientist (1773–1857) who worked on the theory of glider flight, built a model glider and produced a larger machine that could carry a human being. His studies inspired later pioneers such as Otto Lilienthal of Germany.

Isambard Kingdom Brunel A British engineer (1806–1859) who built tunnels and bridges and the Great Western Railway. He is best known for his three remarkable steamships: the *Great Western* (1837), the *Great Britain* (1843) and the *Great Eastern* (1858).

Etienne Lenoir A French engineer (1822–1900) who invented a stationary gas engine which burned coal gas – the first internal combustion engine.

Werner von Siemens A German industrialist and inventor (1816–1892) who developed electric railways, and also lighting and telegraphs. His brother **William** (1823–1883) invented a new steel-making process, and settled in Britain.

James Starley A British engineer (1831–1881) who built sewing machines and improved bicycles with gears. He began building Ariel bicycles in 1871.

John Boyd Dunlop A Scottish inventor (1840–1921) who was the first manufacturer of inflated (air-filled) rubber tyres.

Charles Parsons A British engineer (1854–1931) who built the first steam turbine engine for ships. Steam turbines were later used in power stations to generate electricity.

Gottlieb Daimler A German engineer (1834–1900) who built a motor bicycle and a car in 1886, and was one of the pioneers of automobile development.

Karl Benz A German engineer (1844–1929) who built the world's first motor-car driven by a petrol engine. He and Gottlieb Daimler were the 'fathers' of the motor-car.

Ferdinand von Zeppelin A German engineer (1838–1917) who built airships which from 1900 to the 1930s bore his name and were the largest ever made.

John P. Holland An American engineer (1841–1914) who built the first reliable submarine in 1897. It had petrol and electric engines and was bought by both the British and the US navies.

Rudolph Diesel A German engineer (1834–1913) who turned from refrigerators to engines, developing the oil-fuelled engine that bears his name.

Wilbur Wright An American inventor (1867–1912) who with his brother **Orville** (1871–1948) ran a bicycle shop in Dayton, Ohio. Self-taught, they built the *Flyer,* which in 1903 made the first flight by a winged, heavier-than-air machine under its own power.

▲ **Henry Ford with his first car.**

Henry Ford An American industrialist (1863–1947) who built the first mass production car, the Model T, on an assembly line. The car was produced at a price ordinary people could afford, was robust and easy to drive. He later built aircraft and tractors.

Frank Whittle A British engineer (1907–) who developed the theory of the jet engine and patented a gas-turbine jet in 1930. His engine was ground-tested in 1937 but did not fly in a plane until 1941.

Igor Sikorsky A Russian inventor (1889–1972) who emigrated to the USA in 1919. He founded the Sikorsky Aero Engineering Corporation in 1923, and designed the first single-rotor helicopter in 1939.

Robert Watson-Watt A British scientist (1892–1973) who developed radar (radio direction finding) in the 1930s. It was first used to detect enemy bombers during the Second World War, but has since become an essential navigation aid for ships and aircraft.

Sergei Korolyov A Ukrainian-born engineer (1906–1966) who developed the USSR's rocket programme. Working on captured German V2 rockets in the late 1940s he built the huge rockets that gave the USSR an early lead in the 'space race'. His Vostok rockets launched the first space satellites and the world's first astronaut, Yuri Gagarin.

☀ GLOSSARY 1

A ready-reference guide to many of the terms used in this book.

Airship An aircraft filled with a lighter-than-air gas, such as helium or hydrogen. Unlike balloons, they have engines driving propellers, and are usually cigar- or sausage-shaped, rather than spherical.

Apollo The name given to the American moon-flight programme. Seven Apollo moon-landings were made from 1969 to 1972.

Archimedean screw A spiral screw turned by a crank handle inside a casing, originally used to lift water for irrigation. It is thought to have been invented by the Greek mathematician, Archimedes, about 287-212 BC.

Battery An electrical cell which uses chemical reactions to make electricity.

Carburettor This is the part of a petrol engine that mixes air with petrol to form an explosive vapour. The vapour is let into the cylinder, where it is ignited by a spark from the spark plug.

Carrack Sailing ship of the 1400s, with three masts carrying square and lateen sails.

Coal gas Gas made by distilling or heating coal. It is mainly methane, hydrogen and carbon monoxide. Used for heating and lighting from the 1800s, but now largely replaced by natural gas.

Container A large metal box in which factory goods are packed before shipment. The container can be carried by road or rail, in large aircraft or on the decks of special ships. The cargo remains inside until the container reaches its destination.

Crankshaft In a steam or petrol engine, this is linked by connecting rods to the piston. The sliding rods convert one kind of motion to another. As the piston goes up and down, the crankshaft is turned round and round.

Cylinder A hollow tube in an engine, inside which a piston moves up and down with a pumping action.

Diesel engine An internal combustion engine in which fuel is ignited by hot compressed air, not by spark plugs. It is named after its inventor, Rudolph Diesel.

Distributor This part of a petrol engine sends high-voltage electrical current from the coil to each spark plug in turn.

Economics The science that studies the production, distribution and consumption of wealth.

Expansion Spreading out or taking up more space. Gases and many other substances expand when heated.

Flywheel A spinning wheel fixed to the crankshaft of a petrol engine. It stores enough energy during the power stroke to carry the crankshaft through the other strokes (*see* **Stroke**). Flywheels were also used in steam engines, to do the same job.

Friction A force created when two objects or substances rub together. Lubrication (oiling or greasing moving parts) and bearings (metal balls rolling between the parts) help to reduce friction.

Galleon A type of sailing ship developed in the 1500s, which was larger and faster than the earlier cog and carrack. Galleons had three or four masts. Their design changed comparatively little from 1600 to 1800.

Gas One of the three forms of matter (the others are solid and liquid). A gas has no fixed shape or volume, and expands to fill any container.

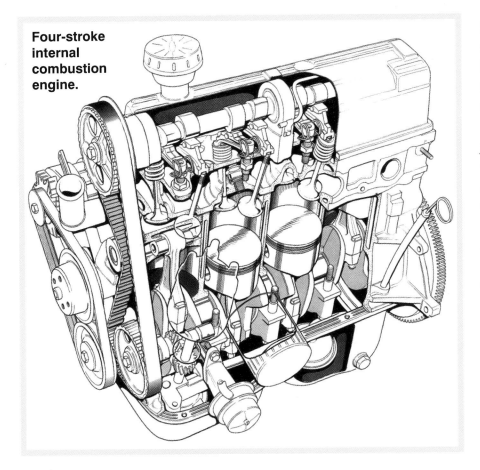

Four-stroke internal combustion engine.

Internal combustion engine An engine that burns petrol or fuel oil inside a cylinder to produce motion that is transmitted by a shaft driving wheels or propellers.

Internet A worldwide computer web, through which users can send and receive information by way of telephone lines and satellites.

Jet This is a fast-moving stream of air, gas or water. A jet engine burns fuel, and shoots out hot exhaust gases – this force pushes the engine in the opposite direction.

Kayak A canoe used by Arctic Inuit people. It is made from sealskin stretched over a frame, and paddled along.

Lateen sail A triangle-shaped sail first used by Arab and Asian sailors, and in the 1400s copied by European shipbuilders.

Liquid fuels These are the preferred fuels for space rockets, although solid-fuel boosters are used during launching of some rockets. The liquid is a chemical mixture. The Saturn V moon rocket burned a mixture of liquid oxygen and liquid hydrogen.

Nuclear power The harnessing of the energy of nuclear fission (atom splitting) in a reactor so that it can be used to do work. The energy can be used to heat water to make steam to drive turbine engines, for example as in a nuclear power station or nuclear submarine.

Gauge The distance between inside edges of railway track. Standard railway gauge in the USA, Britain and most of Europe, is 1435 millimetres (4 feet 8½ inches).

Gears Wheels with cogs or teeth that mesh with one another.

Glider An aircraft with wings but no engine. The glider is heavier than air, and cannot take off on its own. It has to be launched by being towed or catapulted, but can then gain height by soaring on rising currents of warm air. Model gliders and gliders from which a person dangled (like a modern hang-glider) were used in early aviation experiments in the 1800s.

Gravity Force of attraction between objects. The planets and the stars pull objects near to them, towards their centres.

Hull This is the main body of a ship. Modern hulls are made from welded steel sections.

Ignition system An electrical circuit which uses power from a battery to make a spark. This explodes fuel mixture inside a petrol engine.

Industrial Revolution A change in society by which many people move from agriculture to factory work. In Britain it began in the second half of the eighteenth century spreading to Europe and the US in the nineteenth century.

Patent A document in which an inventor describes a new invention, and claims sole rights to make, use and sell it.

Periscope An optical instrument which is a tube with reflecting mirrors either end. It can be raised from a submarine under water to give a view above the surface.

Petrol (gasoline) A fuel burned in car engines that is a mixture of chemicals called hydrocarbons, made from refined petroleum oil.

Pneumatic tyre The first bicycles and cars had wooden or metal wheels with hard rims and later solid rubber tyres. The air-filled pneumatic tyre was available from the 1880s.

Propeller Device with blades set at angles around a shaft. All airplanes had spinning propellers (airscrews) before 1939. Ships are driven by large screws, which turn more slowly in the water. Some hovercraft also have airscrews.

Radar This stands for Radio Detection And Ranging. It is a device that sends out radio waves and picks up reflected echoes from objects. It is used for air and sea navigation, for military target detection, and air-traffic control.

Rudder This is a vertical blade fastened to the stern of a ship. When the rudder is moved, the ship turns left or right.

Snorkel A breathing tube in a submarine, which sticks up above the water while the rest of the submarine is submerged. It takes in fresh air and gets rid of stale air and fumes.

Sonar This stands for 'sound navigation and ranging'. It is a device for detecting underwater objects through reflected sound waves – also known as echo-sounding.

Space station A permanent base in orbit around the Earth that is assembled from sections brought up by rocket. It is used by visiting astronauts for scientific and engineering research in space.

Spark plug A device used in petrol engines which makes a spark jump across a gap when a strong electric current passes through it. The spark ignites a fuel and air mixture.

Steam engine An engine in which water is heated in a boiler to make steam. The steam is then used at high pressure to drive pistons linked by rods to the drive wheels of factory machines or vehicles.

▲ The Mir space station has been in orbit around the Earth since 1986. It is visited by teams of astronauts who carry out experiments in space.

Stroke A stroke is the movement of a piston inside the cylinder of an engine. A four-stroke engine has four sequences: suction when fuel enters the cylinder; compression when it is squeezed; ignition when it is set alight; and exhaust which removes the waste gases.

Transmission system This transmits or links the motion of the engine to the drive wheels. The up and down action of the pistons is converted into the rotary motion of the wheels.

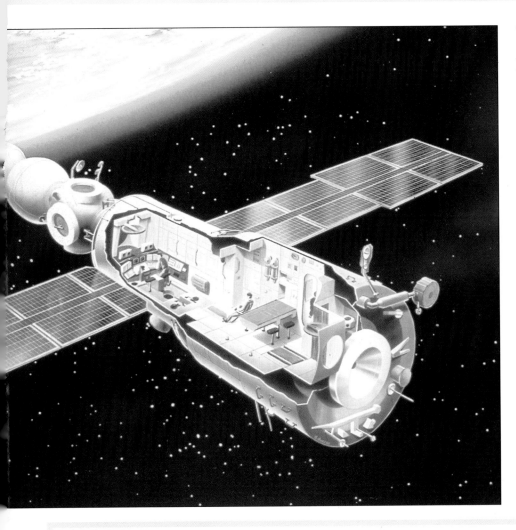

Turbine An engine in which a flow of steam, water or gas spins blades fixed to a shaft. Gas turbines are used in ships and jet planes. Steam turbines are used in ships.

Vacuum A space from which air or other gas is removed. A railway vacuum brake is held off by very low air pressure (a near vacuum) and put on when air is allowed in.

Valve A device that lets a substance flow one way only – for instance, an inlet valve lets the air-fuel mixture into the cylinder of a petrol engine.

Wind tunnel A device in which aircraft or rocket designs in model form are tested. A fan blows air around the model, so that the model's behaviour at different speeds can be studied.

GOING FURTHER

Books Your local library and bookshop should have a range of excellent, illustrated information books on transport, mostly on particular areas – such as ships, railways, aviation. Fewer books look at transport from the overall historical and social aspect. You might like to look out for the following: *Fantastic Transport Machines* by Chris Oxlade, Watts 1994; *Trains and Railways* in the *Windows on the World* series, Dorling Kindersley 1992; also in *The Visual Dictionary of* series: *Cars*; *Ships and Sails*, and *Flight* also published by Dorling Kindersley.

Magazines Special-interest weekly or monthly magazines on railways, cars, boats and aircraft can be found in almost every newsagent. General-interest science magazines such as *New Scientist* contain items on inventions and technological developments.

Places In Britain, the Science Museum in London has a world-famous collection of transport items, including engines, with models. There are historic aircraft and car collections, such as the Royal Air Force Museum at Hendon and the National Motor Museum at Beaulieu. Regional museums include Belfast's Transport Museum and the Museum of Science and Industry in Birmingham. The National Railway Museum is in York. The National Maritime Museum in London covers the history of ships, and Bristol is home to the National Life-Boat Museum.

CD-ROM Multimedia encyclopedias such as *Microsoft Encarta* and the *Grolier Encyclopedia* contain general information on transport. Koch Media have a motor-car title: *100 Years of Motoring*.

INDEX

Numbers in **bold** refer to pictures or drawings as well as text.

air show **24**
airplane 5, 17, **24-25**, 27, **32**, 33, 35, 40
airships **16-17**
Aldrin, Edwin 39
American War of Independence 26
animals **4**, 9
Armstrong, Neil 39

balloons **16-17**
Benedictus, Edouard 29
Benz, Berta 23
Benz, Karl 17, **22-23**, 43
Bernoulli, Daniel 18
bicycles **20-21**, **23**, 25
boats **6-7**, **12-13**, **18-19**, 45
Braun, Werner von 38, 39
Brindley, James 12
Brunel, Isambard Kingdom 18, 19, 36, 42
buses **28-29**, **40**
Bushnell, David 26

canals **12-13**, 36, 42
cars 5, 9, 17, **22-23**, 28-29, 36, **40**, **41**, 43
carts 4, 5, 8, 9
Cavendish, Henry 16
Cayley, George 24, 42
Charles, Jacques 16
Chinese junk **10**
Columbus, Christopher 10, 11
container port **37**
Ctesibius of Alexandria 12
Cugnot, Nicolas 13

Daimler, Gottlieb 17, 22, 43

Diesel, Rudolf 30, 43
Drebbel, Cornelis van 26
Dunlop, John Boyd 20, 43

Egyptians 7, 9
boats **6-7**
chariots **8**, 9
Rameses II **8**
engines 12, 13, **14**, 15, 16, 17, 18, 19, **22-23**, 25, 27, 30, **32-33**, 37, 39, 44, **45**, 46

First World War 17, 25, 27, 37
Fitch, John 13
Focke, Heinrich 34
Ford, Henry 28, 29, **43**
Ford Motor Company 29
Franklin, Benjamin 24
fuels 5, 14, 18, 22, 30, 36, 37, **38**, 40, 45, 46
Fulton, Robert 13, 26, **42**

Gargarin, Yuri **38**
Giffard, Henri 17
gliders 24, 25, 39, 45
Goddard, Robert 38
Greek warship **6**

Harrison, John 11
helicopters 25, **34-35**, air-sea rescue **34**, 35
Heyerdahl, Thor 7
Holland, John 27, 43
hydrofoil **41**

Industrial Revolution 12, 13, 14, 18, 45
iron 18, 19

Kennedy, John F. 39
kites 24, 25
Korolyov, Sergei 43

Lenoir, Etienne 22, 43

Leonardo da Vinci 34, 42
Levassor, Emile 28
Lilienthal, Otto 24
locomotives 5, **14**, 15, **30**, 31, 42
diesel **30-31**

McAdam, John 9
Middle Ages 9, 10, 12, 34
Montgolfier Brothers 16, 42

navigation 11
Newcomen, Thomas 12
Newton, Isaac 42

Ohain, Pabst von 32
Otto, Nikolaus 22

paddle-wheels 18, 19
Parsons, Charles 19, 43
pollution 5, 40, 41
power **4-5**, 9, 12, 27, 31, **40**, 45

radar 27, 46
railways **14-15**, 19, 30, 31, 37, 40, 43
underground 31
roads 9, 28, 29
highways **5**
motorways **29**, 37
rockets **38**, 39, 47
Romans 7, 9, 42
Rozier, Jean de 16

satellites 38, 39
Savery, Thomas 12
Second World War 27, 29, 33, 38
ships 6, 7, **10-11**, **18-19**, 26, 27, **36**, 37, 40, 44, 45, 46, 47
Siemens, Werner von, 30, 43
William von 43
Sikorsky, Igor 34, 43
Smith, Francis 18

space shuttles **39**
space stations 39, **46-47**
Starley
James 20, 43
John 20
Stephenson
George 15, 42
Robert 15, 42
Stone Age 4, 8
submarines **26-27**, 35, 46
supersonic speed 33, 38
Symington, William **12-13**

Telford, Thomas 12
trams 29, 30
Trevithick, Richard **14**, 42
Tsiolkovski, Konstantin 38
tyres 9, 20, **23**, 28, 46

Verne, Jules 38
Viking longships 10

wagons **9**
Watson-Watt, Robert 43
Watt, James **13**, 42
wheels 4, 6, 8, 9, 15, 20, 21, 22, 23, 45, 46
Whittle, Frank 32, 43
Wright, Benjamin **13**
Wright
Orville 25, 43
Wilbur 25, 43

Zeppelin, Ferdinand von 17, 43